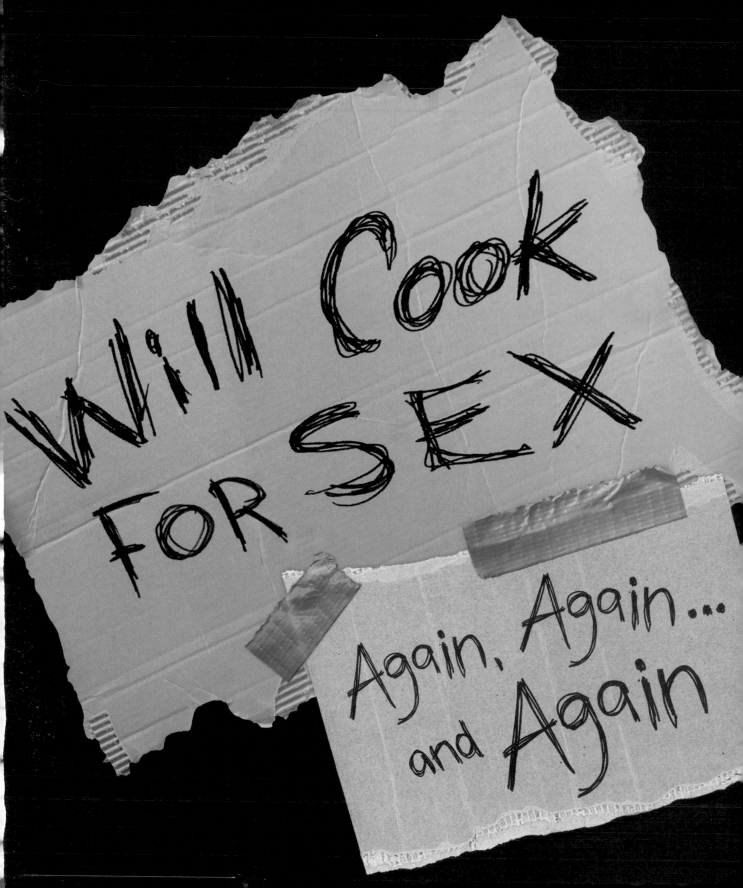

Will Cook for SEX

Again, Again... and Again

A Guy's Guide to Cooking
Intermediate Edition

Rocky Fino

STEPHENS PRESS, LLC
A Stephens Media Company

LAS VEGAS, NEVADA

Editor: Heidi Knapp Rinella

Photography: Ignite Design and Advertising

Creative Direction/Design: Chris Wheeler

Cover Model: Kim Wheeler

Cataloging in Publication

Fino, Rocky.

Will cook for sex again, again, and again : a guy's guide to cooking — intermediate edition /
Rocky Fino.

176 p. : photos ; 24 cm.

ISBN: 1-935043-18-8

ISBN-13: 978-1-935043-18-8

The second cookbook written for men who seek to impress a woman with prowess in the kitchen.

1. Cookery. I. Title.

641.5 dc22   2010   2010921826

A Stephens Media Company

POST OFFICE BOX 1600, LAS VEGAS, NEVADA 89125-1600

stephenspress.com

Printed in Hong Kong

Here's to good food, fine wine... and gettin' naked thereafter!

Rocky

To my friends who continue to support the effort, and to all of the new friends that I have met since the release of Will Cook for Sex. Your stories and enthusiasm are the true success of the project.

Cheers!
Rocky

perseverate \per-sev-uh-reyt\, verb:
1. to repeat something insistently or redundantly.

Dear Rocky,

*I just want you to know that after 14 years of marriage, and my begging and enticing my husband, Steve, to cook with me (if not for me) but to NO avail, he stumbled upon your book, **Will Cook for Sex**, in a wine shop and it is the only cook book that would ever have caught his attention and he has finally stepped foot into the kitchen!!! Not only cooking wonderful food, but your easy step by step recipes look and taste like a gourmet meal!*

Thank you from the bottom of my heart!

Carie

Contents

A Foreword from the Author's Mother

It is said that there are two sides to every story and that no two people recall an event the same. That is never more evident than with my two parents. I have created these books with help from my old man and provided his perspective of my upbringing in the foreword of the original Will Cook for Sex.

I never mentioned my mother's contribution. Quite frankly, it didn't bother her to remain detached from her son's efforts to score. To her credit, she also did a fair amount of the cooking in our household especially Monday through Thursday for the four kids. So I figured that is was only natural to give her point of view for the foreword to the follow up. The Old Man was not as keen on the idea.

YOUR MOTHER?

I was raised by Mother, Rocky's grandmother, who was ahead of her time. She worked, and wore slacks and nail polish, which at the time, were considered shameful acts of a "modern woman". But, more substantively, she knew the importance of healthy, organic food and prepared our meals accordingly.

Combine that upbringing with my doctor who said to me while pregnant with all my kids, "if it tastes good, spit it out," and my palate and those of my children have no affinity for processed food. This would haunt me later especially by the last child when I would have appreciated getting by with a substandard TV dinner; but Rocky would not tolerate any packaged food. I was probably the only mom on the block wishing her kid on occasion did not demand fresh meats, vegetables, and fruits.

Admittedly, my food was more functional than flamboyant, that was until I married an aspiring chef disguised as an accountant (The Old Man). Suddenly, food was not only a means to a healthy end, but the main attraction; and to run out of food for your guests, the ultimate sin. To this day, I have visions of the back of a feverous chef tossing romaine trims over his shoulder while the kids clamored to clean up behind him. Name a date or holiday, and anyone of us could recall the food that made it memorable. Together, our kids were taught food must taste good, look good and be good for you, an alluring combination.

The only problem was many of the big feasts, were for men-only affairs. Rocky, lacking the mechanical inclinations of his older brother, was known for his keen observation. While he could hang with the boys, he quickly surmised, why limit the magic of food to family functions and moments of male-bonding. This was a serious underutilization of this delectable skill. If luck is when opportunity meets experience, for Rocky, getting lucky is creating an opportunity from his experiences. Perks, you could say, of being a "modern man". What a difference a generation makes.

— MJ

"I recall that he ate anything in sight, including the packaging."

— The Old Man

Introduction

Impressing your woman is a never-ending affair.

There are two common misconceptions about cooking for sex. The first is that this is a young man's game. I worked on the first book with my old man. When we were working on the drafts and recipes, I saw many of his friends, who obviously are older, get genuinely excited about the idea. They couldn't wait to try the recipes and on more than one occasion would call for cooking advice leading into an evening. That's a rather small sample of a generation so I couldn't hang my theory on their enthusiasm, but once the book was released, there was no doubt who was enthusiastic about cooking for sex. The 50-, 60- and 70-somethings enjoyed the idea as much as the 20- and 30-year-olds! The Who got it wrong; you don't want to die before you get old.

The other misconception is that this is merely a maneuver for single guys. Not necessarily. We're always trying to score with our women, and that applies to married men just the same. Cooking for your mate is a fail-safe approach to impressing her, thus making you more attractive in her eyes and inevitably setting the mood. I have met countless wives who are thrilled about their men cooking for them.

No man's theory goes unchallenged. I've taken numerous punches from the naysayers, yet I continue to believe that everyone can use the skill. Some men claim, "I'm married, and she handles all of the kitchen duties." I hope you make decent money, with that old-school mentality. It doesn't work in my world.

Others have said, "I'm single, and I want to remain that way." It doesn't sound like that will be a problem.

Or, "I don't believe in pre-marital sex." I don't believe there needs to be anything "pre-marital" about it. Every guy should show his lady a little attention. What you're looking for in return is your call.

Then there's the macho-guy claim, "I don't need any help getting laid." Really?

Finally, "I'm a vegan." OK, I give. My book doesn't apply to everyone. I'm sure vegans get lucky, just not by way of the kitchen.

Women are like college football boosters: Pull off a big victory and they expect one again next week.

Those punches are from a few of the doubters I've crossed. Many more of you like the idea and appreciate my help. That's why we're back.

If you enjoyed some success from what you learned in *Will Cook for Sex: A Guy's Guide to Cooking*, you know the power that chivalry has with your mate. For those who were encouraged to cook for the first time, I'm certain you surprised her. She didn't see it coming and her expectations were probably low.

Those pleasant surprises are the most successful. It's like a college football coach taking on a losing program: There's nowhere to go but up. The more difficult task is the following season after the turnaround, when expectations are higher. Women are like college football boosters: Pull off a big victory and they expect one again next week. So in our continuous pursuit of her admiration, we must constantly improve upon our game. Thus, the inevitable follow-up. Her expectations are higher, and so should be yours.

The Crossover

You've been a couple, you're part of a couple or you're trying to be a couple. Most of us are covered by these three categories and will find our way into the subsequent chain of important events I've featured in this book — situations in a man's life when it helps to know how to cook.

Although there are major differences in the day-to-day lives of men who are single and men who are married, there is also a tremendous amount of crossover between the two.

Realize that entertaining with food applies to everyone. Single guys can throw a dinner party like married guys can still have a dinner date. The events are interchangeable and relate to all.

The final chapter of this edition is the Little League team party. If you don't have children, it would seem odd to find yourself in the situation of throwing such a party. I agree. But the many of you who do have children will relate to the team party, others can recall the event from their childhood and most will experience it as a parent at some time. So hold onto the book for when that time comes. In the meantime, as with every recipe in the book, use them for whatever occasion you deem appropriate.

Single guys can throw a dinner party like married guys can still have a dinner date.

The Cook

The idea of cooking for my date was not something I dreamed about as a child.

When I was young and ignorant, I never figured on having to work that hard at it. As I grew older and became slightly less ignorant, I discovered that I was admired more in the kitchen than in the bedroom…go figure. So I decided to play my best hand.

I'm not an executive chef — I did not go to culinary school — but a cook just like you. I learned to cook growing up in our kitchen at home and from my old man's cookouts.

I have met many people since *Will Cook for Sex*, and it continues to amaze me how universally intrigued people are with someone who knows how to cook. That appreciation is seen at all levels. I admire what master chefs can do, but also realize you don't need to be a chef to entertain and impress others. A good French-dip lamb sandwich is equally impressive at times.

Once again, this book is the product of my joy for writing and spending time cooking with my old man. Together, we carefully designed the recipes so that the average guy at home could succeed on his first attempt. Since this is the "intermediate edition" there are a couple of new challenges, but the results are worth the effort.

I know from experience that if you cook for her on a regular basis, she naturally begins to take it for granted and does not always reciprocate in the manner you deserve. Sometimes we need to increase our efforts to remind her how fortunate she is.

What You Need:
Extra Equipment

My idea of a good hobby is one you can never stop spending money on. If you're into fishing, cycling, sailing, skiing, golf, etc., you know what I'm talking about. It's exciting to get a new piece of gear and usually gets me fired up to try it. And like all sports or hobbies, the better you get, the more you yearn for better equipment. It enhances your game.

Cooking falls into the same category. You don't need much to get you started (as shown here from *Will Cook for Sex: A Guy's Guide to Cooking*), but as you expand your skills, you need more gear.

Which is not to be confused with gadgets. Golfers know they need good clubs, decent shoes and, in my case, lots of golf balls. What they don't need are any more of the trinkets that already fill the closet, in the form of fifteen years of Father's Day and Christmas gifts from the wife and kids.

The same rule applies to the kitchen. Spare yourself the avocado slicer, mango pitter — unnecessary gadgets that clutter up your utensil drawer. Spend your cash on functional equipment you actually will use.

Here are a few more items you'll need to handle the recipes in this edition:

Ceramic ramekins
Whisk
Spring form pan
Tart pan (9" fluted)
Hand mixer
Pizza trays
Rolling pin
Baking pan (9"x13")

Basic Equipment: Once Again

Many cookbooks assume the reader has a completely outfitted kitchen. When it comes to guys, that's a stupid assumption. Outside of an ESPN feed, nothing should be assumed. A completely outfitted kitchen isn't necessary, anyway. The equipment you need to turn yourself into a cook is minimal and shouldn't cost more than a couple of hundred bucks. It's worth it.

Essential equipment:

- 3 non-stick pans
- Pots – small to large
- Tongs
- A sharp knife
- A spatula
- 2 large spoons (one slotted – the kind with holes)
- A cutting board
- A measuring cup
- Measuring spoons
- Mixing bowls
- A blender
- An apron
- Cookie sheet
- Roasting pan
- Ramekins (small baking bowl)
- A corkscrew

You'll need non-stick skillets in various sizes, and you can buy them as a set. Even cheap ones will do. But any tool that touches the inside of the pan should be plastic or wood, because metal will scratch the finish. Then again, if you buy cheap non-stick pans, and you scratch them, you can buy new ones.

As for the tongs, spring-loaded ones work best.

And get an apron. If you don't, you're going to be doing a lot of laundry, because if nothing else, you'll wipe your hands on your jeans without knowing it. Besides, an apron on a guy — miracle that it is — is a turn-on for many women.

The corkscrew is also essential. There is more to entertaining — and scoring — than cooking.

Optional equipment:
- Extra pans
- Additional knives
- A roasting rack
- A deep pot
- Whisk
- Mallet (wood or steel)
- Corkscrews, corkscrews, and more corkscrews

If you've got a patio, porch or yard, you should have a grill. But if you can't cook outdoors at your place, don't worry about it.

Though the food can stand on its own, decorative plates and serving dishes will make it look classy, and that's a turn-on, too.

As for the corkscrews, my old man always says, "corkscrews are like car keys — you're never sure where you left them." Always have extras.

Wine – The Basics

"A meal without wine is like a day without sunshine."

That phrase was etched on a bottle carriage that sat on our dining room table when I was growing up. I don't know who coined the phrase, but I credit my folks for passing on the wisdom.

Every culinary move that you make to entertain your guest or guests will be enhanced by good wine. Realize that "good wine" is a relative term. If money is no object, selecting a good bottle of wine is not a challenge. But generally money is a concern, so it's best to develop some understanding, because you can't choose wines by the look of their labels. That's similar to dating; you can choose the "pretty label" only to realize once you tried it that it's not very pleasant. It's best to know what's in the bottle.

It is nice to gain some general knowledge and develop a palate for flavors. And as every good coach will agree, the best way to develop these skills is through practice, practice and more practice. You can read up on it and listen to an array of experts, but the whole point is to actually taste it (or drink it, in my case).

Wine is an overwhelming field of study. I find that rather than profess what I know about wine, I prefer to listen to the people who live it — the winemakers, storeowners, distributors and restaurateurs who are around it every day. Take time to learn about wine from these sources. They'll be happy to coach you.

Any experience beyond that is a bonus. Spending the weekend in wine country, going to tastings and attending a food-and-wine expo will only enhance your knowledge and appreciation for good wine.

For those who have been married so long that wine is a hobby the two of you enjoy, then talk away. But don't take that approach with a new date. That's hardly the way to create a smile, and you need to create a smile if you're looking to go for the end zone later.

That's similar to dating; you can choose the "pretty label" only to realize once you tried it that it's not very pleasant.

Warning
When drinking wine together (just the two of you), it should be enjoyed, not talked about. No woman has ever called her friends after a date and boasted, "And he served a full-bodied wine with an aroma of cranberry, notes of cassis and a subtle finish!"

The Date – Revisited

I hope I never outgrow the excitement of a dinner date. It is the quintessential event in the courtship process, and thus deserves another look.

Have you ever noticed how much men and women "play the game" with each other when it comes to relationships? We rarely shoot straight with one another and always are watching the other's next move to try to guess his or her intentions. For women, men are a game. And in return, for us guys, women are a game — a game I liken to golf. Golf is a game that can never be mastered, one you can always improve at, and that plays in streaks that often leave you talking to yourself.

We rarely hit the ball perfectly, but when we do, it's exhilarating. It's that birdie on 18 that allow us to overlook our score on the previous 17 holes and leaves us yearning to play another day.

We tend to stumble through 17 holes of mistakes with our women, too. We rarely make the perfect move with our significant other, but when we do, the joy is undeniable. It's that little smile or the eye she gives when we finally string together something right in her mind that gives us the feeling — the satisfaction — that we pleased her. Knowing this, we all secretly (and sometimes not so secretly) yearn to get better. We even read about it — openly, in the case of golf, not so openly when we sneak a peek at her latest *Cosmo* to see the "Top 10 Things Women Want to Hear to Get Naked."

The hardest shot in golf is the follow-up to the best drive you have ever unleashed — the 300-yarder straight down the throat of the fairway, leaving you with a three-quarters swing wedge to the dance floor. It's unencumbered, a touch shot, a follow up — and a bitch. The euphoria of finally managing to get that

Golf is a game that can never be mastered, one you can always improve at and that plays in streaks that often leave you talking to yourself.

little bastard into the low iron range ends when you line up over that approach shot, because you are not quite sure how you put together the drive and realize that you probably won't do it again before the turn places an insurmountable amount of pressure on this seemingly easy chip shot.

You begin to talk to yourself, then proceed to "chili-dip" it about twelve yards in front of you, once again failing to reach the green in regulation. Stupid game!

When you surprised her with Power Play Pucks from *Will Cook for Sex*, that was the culinary equivalent of the 300-yard drive down the middle of the fairway. Now it's time to follow up with the approach shot. We made great strides in your drive in book one, but by now the ladies have learned that one good drive doesn't make the man. You need to finish the hole.

There are new courses to play in the relationship game, with new dinners she's not expecting. I'm providing some great ideas, ranging from casual evenings spent at home to anniversary moments, dinner with her parents and sweet finishes, because we must continue to work on our game if we're going to shave some strokes off of our score.

An Evening In

This is the most productive date of all. There's no driving involved, no busy restaurants, no distractions. It is, without question, the highest-probability play when hoping to score by the end of the night. Provide a little good food, maybe a movie on the couch and we've got a winner (or at least a 50/50 chance).

It's one thing to set "the mood;" maintaining the mood is an entirely different challenge. The beauty of an evening in is that you can strike when the iron is hot. If that moment comes following the appetizer, forget the meal and cash that ticket; you'll both be hungry later. Realize that setting the mood is an achievement, but the mood is ever so delicate, and we guys are not. As good as we are at bringing our date to that state, we are equally (or more) likely to fumble if too much time is allowed. On a mood-setting breakaway, head straight for the end zone and don't break stride.

A table for two at a swank restaurant doesn't allow for us to play to the impulse. I speak from experience. I once made the mistake of dining out on Valentine's Day at a swank steakhouse. There were smiles and giggles throughout dinner that led to some footsies during dessert. Knowing my own inadequacy at maintaining the mood, I quickly requested the check.

During the time for the credit card to be processed, coat check, hustling the valet, managing the short drive home, parking, busting in the door and kicking off the shoes, the mood went from "I'm hot" to "Where is this relationship going?" Darn! Your answer had better be better than mine was if you think that you're gonna score following that.

If I had wisely chosen an evening in I would've scored before the plates were cleared as the romance of the dinner took effect, most likely having staved off the where-are-we-headed question altogether, or at least having gotten lucky before facing it.

It doesn't have to be an occasion like Valentine's Day. An evening in with dinner should be a frequent part of your schedule. The following recipes are a couple of winning ideas to get you started. From there, you can experiment with other recipes from the book and/or ideas you have discovered on your own.

It's one thing to set "the mood;" maintaining the mood is an entirely different challenge.

SALMON EGG TOASTIES

As grocery stores expand their offerings to add more specialty items, foods like salmon eggs have become more readily available.

INGREDIENTS

Sourdough roll or baguette 1
Avocado .1 medium
Sour cream . . . . 4 teaspoons
Salmon eggs (caviar) . . . . .1 oz.

Step one
- Slice roll or baguette ¼-inch thick.
- Slice avocado ¼-inch thick.

Step two
- Broil or toast bread slices for approximately 1 to 2 minutes.

Step three
- Place slice of avocado on each slice of bread.
- Top with dollop of sour cream.
- Top with salmon eggs.

Step four
- Place on plates.

Serves 2-4

Tip
Crackers can be substituted for rolls or baguette.

PISTACHIO-CRUSTED ACORN SQUASH

INGREDIENTS

Acorn squash 1

Butter . . . . .2 to 3 tablespoons

Pistachio nuts .2 oz.

Salt and pepper . . . . to taste

Step one

- Preheat oven to 400 degrees.
- Cut squash in half and remove seeds.
- Then cut squash in quarters; wrap in aluminum foil.
- Place in oven and cook until soft, about one hour.

Step two

- Melt butter.
- Chop pistachio nuts.

Step three

- Take squash from oven and remove aluminum foil.

Step four

- Top squash with butter, nuts, salt and pepper.

Step five

- Place squash on cookie sheet and broil until crispy, approximately 5 minutes.

Serves 2-4

ROASTED PEPPER SWORDFISH

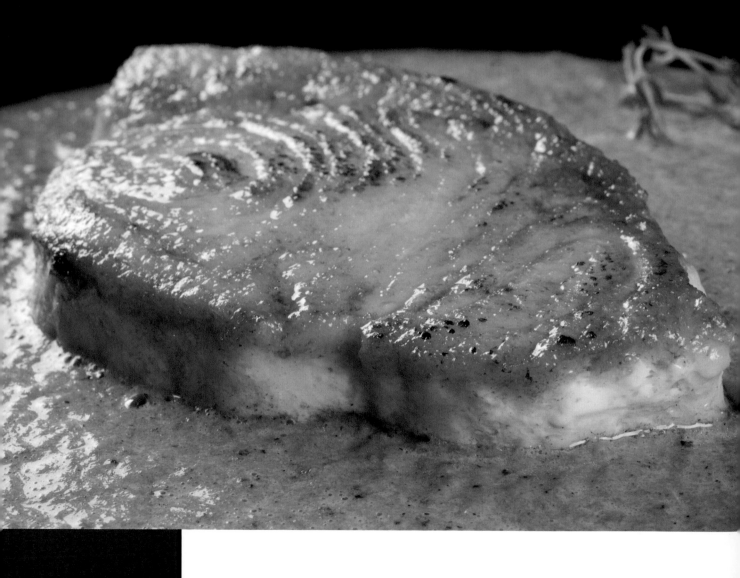

INGREDIENTS

Red bell peppers 2

Onion . . . . 1 medium

Olive oil . . . . 2½ tablespoons

Fresh thyme . . . . 6 sprigs

Vegetable broth . . . . ½ cup

Half and half . . . . 2 tablespoons

Salt and pepper . . . . to taste

Swordfish steaks . . . . 2 (6 to 8 oz. each)

Step one
- Slice peppers and remove seeds.
- Chop onion.

Step two
- Heat 2 tablespoons of oil in large pan.
- Add peppers, onion and thyme.
- Cook over moderate heat until peppers are softened, about 10 minutes.

Step three
- Add vegetable broth and cover.
- Cook until peppers are tender, approximately 8 to 10 minutes.
- Discard thyme and set mixture aside to cool.

Step four
- When cool, transfer ingredients to blender.
- Add half and half and puree for about 10 seconds.
- Add salt and pepper to taste.

Step five
- Heat remaining ½ tablespoon oil in medium pan.
- Add swordfish steaks and cook over medium-high heat until done, turning once (about 8-10 minutes).

Step six
- Transfer swordfish to plate. Serve with red-pepper sauce either on top or in a pool below swordfish.

Serves 2

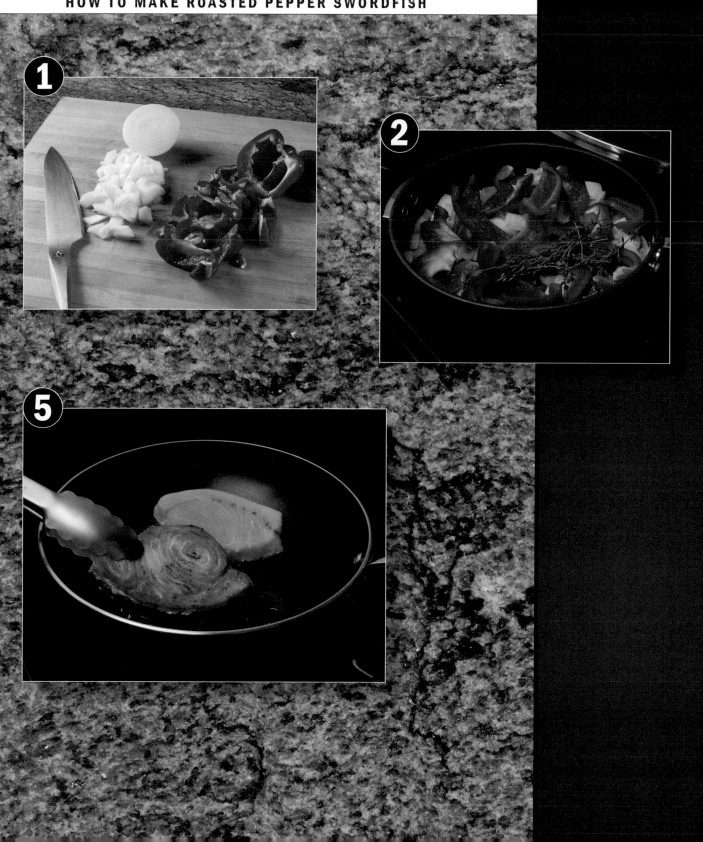

SMOKED SALMON CRISPS

This is a nice upgrade from cheese and crackers, to start the evening.

INGREDIENTS

Sliced smoked salmon . . . . .2 oz.

Shallot 1

Chives. . . . . 10 stems

Sesame seeds . . . . .1 tablespoon

Sour cream . . . . ¼ cup

Thin cocktail crackers 8

Step one

- Finely chop smoked salmon.
- Mince 1 teaspoon each of shallot and chives.
- Snip remaining chives into 1 inch pieces.

Step two

- Combine salmon, shallot, minced chives and sesame seeds in a small bowl.

Step three

- Divide mixture evenly atop crackers.
- Top each with a dollop of sour cream and some snipped chives.

Serves 2-4

Tip
Use black sesame seeds, if available.

SPICY CRAB SALAD

INGREDIENTS

Crabmeat . . . . .4 oz.

Cilantro . . . . 4 sprigs

Red onion .1 small

Avocado . . . . .1 small

Tomato . . . . 1 large

Cayenne pepper . . . . .dash

Lime Vinaigrette:

Olive oil . . . . .2 tablespoons

Fresh lime juice . . . . .2 tablespoons

White wine vinegar . . . . .1 tablespoon

Step one

- Chop 2 tablespoons of cilantro.
- Mince 2 tablespoons of red onion.
- Cut avocado into ½-inch squares.
- Cut two ½-inch slices of tomato.

Step two

Prepare lime vinaigrette

- Mix oil, lime juice and vinegar in a small cup.

Step three

- In a small bowl combine the chopped cilantro, minced red onion, avocado, crabmeat and cayenne.
- Add 2 tablespoons of lime vinaigrette and toss.

Step four

- To serve, place each tomato slice on a plate.
- Top with crab mixture.

Serves 2

POACHED HALIBUT

This is a soup that eats like a meal.

INGREDIENTS

Turnip . . . . .1 medium

Onion. . . . . .1 medium

Parsnip. . . . . .1 large

Carrots . . . . .2 medium

Celery. . . . . 4 stalks

Vegetable broth . . . . 3 cups

Curry powder . . . . ½ teaspoon

Salt and pepper . . . . to taste

Halibut (or sea bass or salmon) . . . . 1 lb., ½-inch-thick slices

Parsley . . . . .10 sprigs

Step one

- Cut turnip, onion, parsnip, carrots and celery into similar-sized chunks and place with the broth in a medium-sized pot.

Step two

- Boil until the vegetables are tender, approximately 30 minutes. Remove from heat and let cool for about 15 minutes.

Step three

- Transfer to blender in stages and puree.

Step four

- Return pureed ingredients to pot and heat over medium flame.
- Add curry powder, salt and pepper and either water or additional vegetable stock if too thick.

Step five

- Pour mixture into a large pan to the depth of about 1 inch and bring to boil over high heat.

Step six

- Place halibut slices in curry mixture and poach until done, approximately 3 minutes.

Step seven

- Transfer to soup bowls, adding just enough curry to cover fish.

Step eight

- Garnish with parsley and serve.

Serves 4

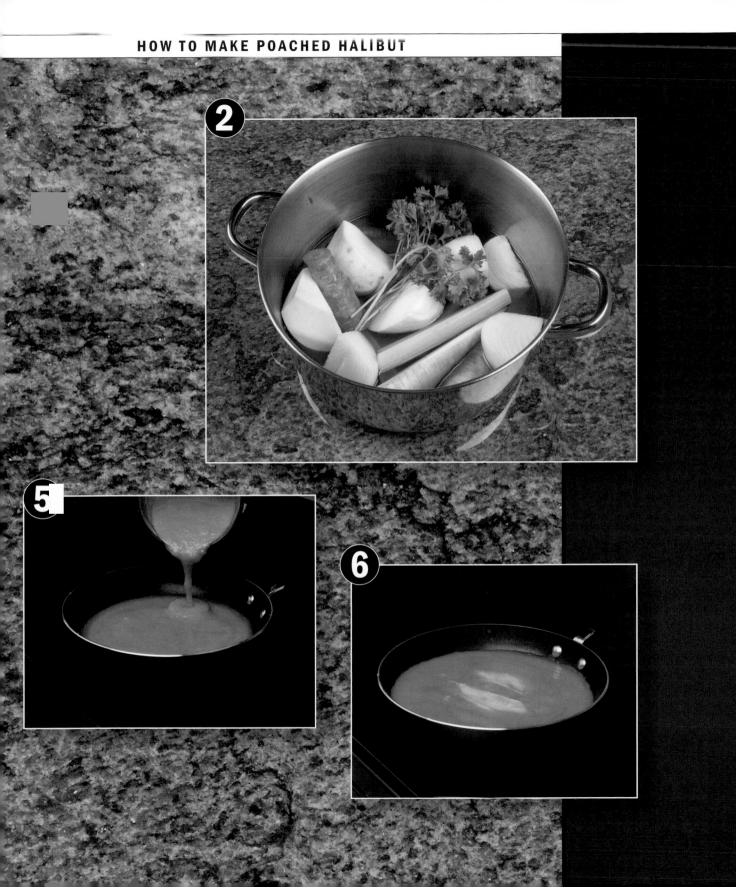

The Anniversary Dinner

Guys take a much simpler approach: The clock starts for me when I score — a second time.

"Come on … I just met her."

Sorry, but any one of us who has dated a girl more than once knows that women get crazy about the idea of commitment to the point where they "memorialize" every moment.

"It's been a month since we first talked on the phone."

"This is our second week together."

Together? I don't even know your last name yet.

It's always difficult to determine the actual "start" date of a relationship. Some start as friendships, two people who hang out in the same group, etc. Other relationships start by rolling over, with a slightly hung-over glaze, and asking the person in your bed, "What was your name again?" Either way, anniversary dates have never been cut and dried in my mind, with the exception of the day you're married. That date is commemorated by matchbooks, candy bags and cocktail napkins – which guys should pin up in their offices so they don't forget the date in the future.

But if you haven't made it to that stage, you have to deal with her zeal for such dates as she promotes bi-weekly updates of anniversarial moments to her friends.

"We went for our third cup of coffee yesterday."

"Did I tell you he sent flowers after our second movie?"

This is their idea of progression. Guys take a much simpler approach: The clock starts for me when I score — a second time.

So whether it's the evening after a "nooner" or your silver anniversary, if she has expressed that the evening is a special anniversary event, you have to perform once again.

Women don't take this date lightly. As a matter of fact, they don't find the humor in your failing to remember. Get to the point where you can narrow it down to a specific date on the calendar. I've given you my line of reasoning, but you can use your own. The key is to get it down to a specific date, then do it up right on that night.

This is a special meal, worth spending a little extra. We're still going to keep it simple, but not typical. On your anniversary she is predisposed to feel romantic about the lug she chose as a mate. You have to capitalize on that predisposition. It's not often that she's willing to overlook all of your shortcomings and be in a romantic mood prior to any effort on your part. Take advantage of the moment, and give her more than she is expecting. This could very well lead to nudity, which instantly puts me in a romantic mood.

A brilliantly forged compilation of approachable recipes that will truly make her leg shake a little bit. What will start out as a dish will most certainly end with a kiss...and quite possibly the ultimate dessert.

— Chef J. Geoffrey Johnson, Chef/Restauranteur

CALAMARI —
BEHIND THE BATTER

INGREDIENTS

Cleaned fresh squid . . . . ½ lb.
Garlic . . . . 1 clove
Parsley . . . . 2 sprigs
Basil . . . . 4 basil
Olive oil . . . . 1½ tablespoons
Soy sauce . . . . 2 teaspoons
Salt . . . . to taste
Lemon . . . . ½, cut in wedges

Step one

- Cut body of squid in half length-wise and discard tentacles.
- Mince garlic and parsley.
- Chop basil.

Step two

- Heat oil in a small pan.
- Add garlic and cook for 30 seconds over high heat.
- Add squid and cook for approximately 2 to 3 minutes, stirring occasionally.
- Add basil, soy sauce and salt and stir.
- Remove from heat when squid is done.

Step three

- Serve with lemon wedges and sprinkle with parsley.

Serves 2

TOMATO STACK

INGREDIENTS

Vine-ripened tomatoes	2 large
Avocado	1 medium
Red onion	1 small
Sliced almonds or chopped walnuts	2 oz.
Sour cream	1 tablespoon
Olive oil	1 tablespoon
Blue cheese, crumbled	1½ tablespoons
Milk	2 tablespoons
Cilantro, minced	4 sprigs
Salt and pepper	to taste

Step one

- Slice tomatoes approximately ½-inch thick.
- Cut avocado into ½-inch squares.
- Cut red onion into ⅛-inch slices and then into quarters.

Step two

- To prepare dressing, combine sour cream, olive oil, blue cheese, milk and cilantro in a small bowl.
- Mix with whisk or fork until smooth.

Step three

- Place a tomato slice on a small plate.
- Sprinkle evenly with salt and pepper.
- Top with a few onion slivers, avocado squares and almonds or walnuts.
- Repeat layers 2-3 times.
- Drizzle dressing over top and serve

Serves 2

1

Tip
If available, use three heirloom tomatoes for enhanced presentation.

BROILED LOBSTER TAILS

INGREDIENTS

Raw lobster tails . . . . 2 8-oz.

Parsley . . . . .4 sprigs

Butter, melted . . . . 3 tablespoons

Lemon . . . . 1 wedge

Step one

- Cut lobster tails in half.
- Cut lemon wedges.
- Mince 2 sprigs of parsley.
- Place tails on cookie sheet, shell side down.
- Top with 2 tablespoons of melted butter.

Step two

- Preheat broiler to 450 degrees.
- Place lobster tails approximately 6 inches below heat source.
- Cook until done, approximately 5 minutes.

Step three

- Remove from broiler.
- Top with remaining melted butter and minced parsley.

Step four

- Place on plates and garnish with remaining parsley sprigs.

If desired, serve with Lemon Crème Fettucine (next recipe).

Serves 2

LEMON CRÈME FETTUCINE

INGREDIENTS

Dry fettuccine . . . . 4 oz.

Olive oil . . . . 2 tablespoons

Flour . . . . 1 teaspoon

Lemon . . . . Juice of ½ small

Cream . . . . ¼ cup

Parmesan cheese . . . . . 2 tablespoons grated

Lobster tails . . . . (see previous recipe)

Parsley . . . . 2 sprigs

Salt . . . . 1 tablespoon

Step one

- About 15 minutes before serving, add salt to 2 quarts of water and bring to a boil.
- Add fettuccine and boil until done, approximately 6-8 minutes.

Step two

- In a medium pan, heat olive oil over medium flame.
- Add flour and stir.
- Add 1 tablespoon lemon juice.
- Slowly add cream while stirring.
- Add Parmesan cheese.
- Bring to a boil, then set aside.

Step three

- Add cooked fettuccine to sauce and gently stir.
- Using large-pronged serving fork, roll up half of the fettuccine.

Step four

- Hold the serving fork perpendicular to the plate.
- Remove fork, leaving a stack of fettuccine.

Step five

- Add broiled lobster tails.
- Garnish with parsley and serve.

Serves 2

Her Parents are Coming Over

Caution! This has all of the potential to be a lose-lose situation. There are two certainties — that her parents don't trust their daughter's decision-making, and that they trust your intentions even less.

"I met a guy. He's not much of a looker, not very ambitious, a little overweight and snores loud, but I'm not getting any younger and you gotta take what you can get. Can't wait for you to meet him."

I can only base my opinion on experience. I've yet to impress any of my dates' parents. When I had no money and no job, they didn't trust me. When I had some money and a good job, they didn't trust me. I now spend my time writing books about using food to get laid — and again, no trust. I'll never win them over.

Your goal here is to "underwhelm" them.

What?

Yes, underwhelm them. You seek to overwhelm your date, but look to underwhelm her parents. Remember, if she's excited about you enough for you to meet her parents, then she's already inadvertently set you up for failure by promoting all of your talents and strong points, while avoiding any of your flaws.

There is nothing more dangerous than over-promotion, and we all stand victim to it in the beginning. You never hear of a girl calling up her parents and saying, "I met a guy. He's not much of a looker, not very ambitious, a little overweight and snores loud, but I'm not getting any younger and you gotta take what you can get. Can't wait for you to meet him."

She chooses to avoid any flaws and strictly promote your qualities, which is why her parents have their guard up. They're skeptical, and if you try to impress them with an elaborate meal, they will immediately get turned off by this "slick Willy" boyfriend who has their daughter conned.

Let's do our best to comfort them. As uncomfortable as this is for you — and her — it's equally uncomfortable for them. Let's give them a good, home-cooked meal. That sounds stupid, considering that every recipe in this book is intended to be cooked at home, but I'm referring to an upgraded family-style comfort meal.

This meal should not be served in courses — again, potentially too flashy — but like old-school home cooking, all at once. Nothing exotic. Familiarity creates comfort.

You seek to overwhelm your date, but look to underwhelm her parents.

Good food and great sex are a necessity. Both should be available at all times for the partaking.

— Chef Barry Sexton,
Opinionated Palate

Warning
I've always been a proponent of the apron, and contend that a man in an apron is a turn-on to her. Not so with her dad. Lose the apron on this evening. He's already judging your every move; no need to establish any prejudgment regarding your manhood.

RUSSET SCRAPS

INGREDIENTS

Russet potatoes	3 pounds
Canola oil	1 cup
Salt and pepper	to taste
Sour cream	½ cup
Horseradish	2 tablespoons
Chive minced	8 stems

Step one

- Cut thick peelings from potatoes, approximately ½ wide.
- Preheat oven to 350 degrees.

Step two

- Heat oil in medium pot over medium flame to 350 to 375 degrees.
- Fry potato skins in small batches until brown, approximately 2 to 3 minutes.
- Transfer to cookie sheet lined with paper towels to absorb excess oil.
- Lightly salt and pepper.

Step three

- Remove paper towels and place scraps in oven for 4 to 5 minutes.
- Remove from oven and let cool.

Step four

- Combine sour cream, horseradish, and chives.

Step five

- Place scraps on plates and serve with topping.

Note

You can substitute other high-temperature oils. Olive oil will work, but it's not preferred. And waste not, want not: Save remaining peeled potatoes, covered in water, for later use.

Serves 4

BRUSSELS SPROUT SALAD

The Brussels sprout has been notorious as the bitter green vegetable that you were forced to eat as a child to earn dessert. Blanching the leaves creates a chewy texture and mild flavor that works great for a new salad experience.

INGREDIENTS

Brussels sprouts . . . . 1 pound
Fennel. . . . . .1/2 bulb
Craisins . . . . ¼ cup
Yellow raisins. . . . . ¼ cup
Sunflower seeds . . . . ¼ cup
Feta cheese. . . . . ¼ cup crumbled

Orange Vinaigrette:

Olive oil . . . . .2 tablespoons
Juice from orange . . . . .2 tablespoons
White wine vinegar . . . . .1 tablespoon

Step one
• Separate sprout leaves and discard cores.
• Slice fennel bulb crosswise into 1/8-inch slices.

Step two
• Bring water to boil in large pot.
• Add leaves and blanch until tender, approximately 1 minute.

Step three
• Remove leaves from water and transfer to refrigerator to cool (this step can be done ahead of time).

Step four
Prepare orange vinaigrette
• Mix olive oil, orange juice and vinegar in a small cup.

Step five
• Toss all ingredients with vinaigrette and serve.

Serves 4

POTATO AND CAULIFLOWER PUREE

INGREDIENTS

Russet potatoes	3 large
Cauliflower	1 head
Parsley	4 sprigs
Sliced almonds	1 cup
White bread	2 slices
Garlic	3 cloves
Cream	1 cup
Salt and Pepper	to taste

Step one

- Peel potatoes and cut in quarters.
- Break cauliflower head into florets and discard leaves.
- Mince parsley for garnish.
- Remove crust from bread.

Step two

- Boil potatoes and cauliflower until soft, approximately 30 minutes.
- Drain.
- Mash potatoes and cauliflower.

Step three

- Preheat oven to 400 degrees.
- Place almonds on cookie sheet and toast, approximately 5 minutes.

Step four

- Place bread, garlic and cream in saucepan and cook over low heat for 5 minutes.

Step five

- Put all ingredients except parsley in blender and puree
- Salt and pepper to taste.
- Place in serving bowl and garnish with parsley.

Serves 6

LAMB SHANKS

INGREDIENTS

Flour	½ cup
Salt and pepper	to taste
Lamb shanks	4
Onion	1 medium
Olive oil	2 to 3 tablespoons
Beef broth	3 cups

Step one

- Flour, salt and pepper lamb shanks on all sides.
- Cut onion in approximately ½-inch squares.

Step two

- Heat 1 tablespoon olive oil in large pan.
- Add onion and cook over medium heat for approximately 5 minutes.
- Remove from heat.

Step three

- Heat 1 tablespoon olive oil in a separate pot.
- Brown shanks on all sides, removing them as they're browned (and adding more oil if necessary).

Step four

- Once all shanks have been browned, return them to the pot.
- Add the sautéed onions and the beef broth.
- Bring to a boil, cover, reduce heat and simmer until lamb shanks are tender, approximately 2½ hours.
- Salt and pepper to taste.

Step five

- Serve on a platter or individual plates atop potato cauliflower puree (previous recipe).
- The pan juices make a perfect gravy.

Tip

For a smoother gravy, whirl pan juices in a blender.

Serves 4

Overtime (AKA Dessert)

For those nights when the game is still on the line at the end of regulation, you need some final firepower from the bench.

I avoided desserts in *Will Cook for Sex* because of the technical aspects of baking and confectionary. But as your relationship grows, so do her expectations. Thus, grow you should.

> **Women are into sweets; that is the understatement of the book. We get fired up over anything grilled, while dinner merely is the "task" they must endure to get to dessert.**

Women are into sweets; that is the understatement of the book. We get fired up over anything grilled, while dinner merely is the "task" they must endure to get to dessert.

Consider those kinky, edible sex gifts the gals exchange at bachelorette parties and couples showers. You know the stuff — body frostings, love potions, etc. You never see Cajun Fire Hot or Kansas City BBQ flavors in any of those toys. It's always chocolate, vanilla or strawberry delight. I doubt we'll ever get women to get sexually aroused from the smell of hickory- smoked ribs, so we need to add dessert to our playbook.

I did give you one fail-safe dessert in book one, The Closer. The Closer — the Blue Collar Souffle — is your Closer for a reason. He's your go-to guy when the game's on the line. But as we've seen in many epic seven-game series over the years, you've got to have more than one ace in the bullpen when playing against the same opponent for a series of games.

You can't continue to rely on the Blue Collar Souffle night after night, so I've compiled a handful of desserts you guys can handle. Realize that most desserts are winners in her eyes. The challenge here is not what she's going to like, but what we can make. Baking is different than cooking, and baking recipes require a little learning curve to develop the touch needed to succeed.

I've strived to come up with desserts that you will be able to perfect on the first pass, because I guarantee that no guy will prepare any of these desserts for practice. That would be a smart move on our part, but when dealing with women we generally aren't that smart. Knowing that you're most likely going to go for it, I have selected desserts that have the best odds of turning out right on your first attempt — with the exception of the Elvis Pie. You might want to do a trial run with that one.

That would be a smart move on our part, but when dealing with women we generally aren't that smart.

Warning
Using a "prevent defense" — cooking the same dish that you know she likes repeatedly — is playing not-to-lose. You'll get beat in the end. I recommend you broaden your offerings.

CHOCOLATE TART

This tart is rich in chocolate flavor and not overly sweet.

INGREDIENTS

Crust:

Graham crackers 12

Sugar. . . . . ¼ cup

Unsalted butter . . . . 5 tablespoons

Filling:

Heavy whipping cream . . . . 1¼ cups

Bittersweet chocolate (60% cacao). . . . . 10 oz.

Eggs . . . . .2 large

Vanilla extract. . . . . .1 teaspoon

Salt . . . . ¼ teaspoon

Topping:

Bittersweet chocolate . . . . 2 oz.

Whipping cream. . . . . 1 tablespoon

Corn syrup . . . . 1 tablespoon

Water warm. . . . . 2 tablespoons

Fresh berries . . . . .1 package

Special equipment:

You'll need a 9-inch circular tart pan, 1 inch deep (fluted preferred).

Step one

Crust

- Preheat oven to 350 degrees.
- Crush the graham crackers. Mix graham-cracker crumbs with sugar and butter.
- Place in tart pan, pressing evenly onto bottom and sides.
- Bake until golden brown, approximately 8-10 minutes.
- Remove from oven and cool.

Step two

Filling

- Place 1¼ cups cream in a small pan and bring to a boil.
- Chop 10 ounces of the chocolate, place in a bowl, pour cream over and let rest for 5 minutes.
- Gently stir chocolate until smooth.

Step three

- Whisk together eggs, vanilla and salt in a bowl.
- Combine with chocolate mixture.

Step four

- Pour filling into cooled crust.
- Bake for 25 minutes.
- Remove from oven and cool for 1 hour.

Step five

Topping

- Place remaining 2 tablespoons of cream in a small pan and bring to a boil.
- Chop remaining 2 ounces of chocolate and stir into cream until smooth.
- Stir in corn syrup and 2 tablespoons of warm water.

Step six

- Pour topping onto tart, rotating and tilting so topping coats evenly.
- Let stand for 1 hour.

Step seven

Plate for presentation.

Serves 8 to 10

Note

You can make this tart a day ahead; if you do, do not apply the topping, and keep the tart in the refrigerator. When ready to serve, bring to room temperature before applying topping.

STUFFED ROASTED FIGS

INGREDIENTS

Figs 4
Goat cheese . . . . 2 oz.
Honey. . . . . 2 tablespoons
Ground nutmeg . . . . 1/4 teaspoon

Step one

- Cut stems off of figs.
- Quarter figs, cutting only three-quarters down.
- Stuff figs with cheese.

Step two

- Preheat oven to 425 degrees.
- Place figs in lightly oiled pan and put in oven.
- Roast until softened, approximately 12 minutes.

Step three

- Place one fig on each of four plates.
- Drizzle with honey and sprinkle with nutmeg and serve.

Serves 4

TRIED AND TRUE TIRAMISU

This dessert requires a little more shopping than I prefer, but the results are worth it.

INGREDIENTS

Instant espresso powder . . . . 3 tablespoons

Sugar. . . . . ½ cup plus 1 tablespoon sugar (divided use)

Coffee liqueur (such as Tia Maria) . . . . 3 tablespoons

Egg yolks 4

Chocolate liqueur. . . . . 3 tablespoons

Heavy cream . . . . .1 cup

Mascarpone. . . . . 1 pound (2½ cups)

Lady fingers. 36

Cocoa powder. . . . . .1 teaspoon

Special equipment needed:

13-by-9-inch baking pan

Step one

- Bring 2 cups water to a boil.
- Put the water, espresso powder, 1 tablespoon of sugar and coffee liqueur in a small bowl.
- Stir until sugar is dissolved, then cool.

Step two

- Place a small metal mixing bowl on top of a saucepan containing 1 cup of water over low heat.
- In bowl mix eggs yolks, remaining ½ cup sugar and chocolate liqueur.
- Using a handheld mixer or whisk, whip until tripled in volume, approximately 6 to 8 minutes.
- Remove bowl from heat.
- Beat in mascarpone until just combined.

Step three

- In a large bowl, beat cream until stiff, approximately 5 minutes.
- Fold mascarpone mixture into whipped cream gently but thoroughly.

Step four

- Dip both sides of each ladyfinger into the coffee mixture and then use the ladyfingers to line the bottom of the baking pan, with 18 ladyfingers in three rows (trimming edges to fit, if necessary).
- Spread with half of the mascarpone filling.
- Repeat the process, dipping 18 ladyfingers in the coffee mixture and arranging them on top of the filling.
- Spread with remaining filling.
- Dust with cocoa or grated dark chocolate and chill, covered.

Step five

- Let tiramisu stand at room temperature for 30 minutes before serving.
- Dust with more cocoa or chocolate and serve.

Serves 10-12

ELVIS PIE

Elvis made the peanut-butter-and-banana combination famous, and he never had difficulty making the women swoon. You should have no trouble with your date, either, when serving this dessert.

INGREDIENTS

Layer One (Crust)

Graham crackers. 18

Unsalted butter (room temperature) . . . . 1¼ sticks

White sugar . . . . 6 tablespoons

Layer Two

Cream cheese . . . . 3 8-oz. packages

Natural peanut butter. . . . . .1 cup

Sugar. . . . . ¾ cup

Brown sugar . . . . ¼ cup

Vanilla . . . . 2 teaspoons

Sour cream . . . . ½ cup

Eggs . . . . .4 large

Layer Three

Unsalted butter . . . . ½ cup (1 stick)

Brown sugar . . . . ½ cup

Ripe bananas. 4

Layer Four

Heavy cream . . . . .1 cup

Vanilla . . . . 2 teaspoons

Powdered sugar. . . . . 2 tablespoons

Dark chocolate . . . . 1 oz.

Step one

Layer One

- Preheat oven to 350 degrees.
- Crush graham crackers and mix crumbs thoroughly with 1¼ sticks butter and 6 tablespoons sugar.
- Place mixture in springform pan, pressing evenly onto bottom and up side of pan.
- Bake until golden brown, approximately 8-10 minutes.
- Remove from oven and cool on a rack.

Step two

Layer Two

- In a large bowl using a hand blender or whisk, beat cream cheese and peanut butter until smooth.
- Add ¾ cup sugar and ¼ cup brown sugar and beat until fluffy.
- Slowly add eggs and 2 teaspoons vanilla and blend.
- Add sour cream and blend.

Step three

- Pour mixture into crust.

Step four

- Cut two large pieces of aluminum foil.
- Place springform pan in center of foil and fold foil up the sides.
- Place in a larger roasting pan and add enough water to come up 1 inch on the outside of the springform pan.
- Bake until golden brown, approximately 1¼ hours.
- Remove and cool in refrigerator, uncovered, for at least 6 hours.

Step five

Layer Three

- To make banana layer, slice bananas ½ inch thick.
- Place remaining 1 stick butter and remaining ½ cup brown sugar in a large pan over medium heat.
- Whisk until sugar and butter melt and mixture is smooth and caramel-like, approximately 3 to 4 minutes.
- Add banana slices to pan in a single layer and cook for 2 minutes, turning once.
- Using a fork, carefully transfer banana slices to top of cheesecake, arranging in an even layer.
- Return to refrigerator.

Step six

Layer Four

- Place whipping cream, remaining 2 teaspoons vanilla and powdered sugar in mixing bowl.
- Using an electric hand mixer, beat the cream until stiff.

Step seven

- Spread whipped cream on top of bananas.
- To garnish, grate chocolate over top.

Note
Start slowly
and as cream
thickens, turn
the mixer speed
up; it takes 3
or 4 minutes to
whip a cup of
cream.

FOUR CORNERS DESSERT

You've got a huge lead; dinner won her over. Don't get crazy, hold on to the ball, wear down the clock and get her back to the bedroom. No cooking is involved here — just a little chocolate from your stash, some fresh berries and a good glass of red.

INGREDIENTS

Dark chocolate . . . . 1 bar

Ice cream . . . . .1 pint

Fresh mixed berries . . . . 10 ounces

A good red wine . . . . 1 bottle

Step one

- Freeze chocolate for approximately 30 minutes.
- Break into uneven pieces.

Step two

- Scoop ice cream into bowls.
- Top with chocolate and berries.

Step three

- Serve with good red wine for best results.

Serves 2

Her Litmus Test— The Picnic

Women love to test the valor of their man's romance and commitment. They set up situations that are known challenges for us guys, basically to gauge the effort.

In Southern California, it's the afternoon at Disneyland. Disneyland is a wonderland for kids, and the only adults in the park should be accompanying their little ones. But women love to see if you'll succumb to their desires, including standing in line for It's a Small World — even as far as a photo together with Mickey. Breaking through the macho male exterior of her guy by getting him to participate in such events turns her on.

(On the flipside we challenge her just the same — not necessarily as a turn-on for us, more to feel a sigh of relief if she's willing to roll with a four-hour pre-game tailgate followed by a three-hour football game and an all-night brouhaha following the victory.)

But if Disneyland is a select test for a Southern Californian, the picnic is a commitment test throughout the world. If you're in a new relationship, wait for her to suggest a picnic. She will.

This move needs to be played well by you if you plan on moving forward with her. Played wrong it will appear cliché and look like you're trying too hard. If you recommend a picnic, you are trying too hard. This is her call. You just need to be prepared to handle it.

(If you're married, I recommend you take her on a picnic, since you're past the point of being cliché. She'll assume you're covering up for something you've done wrong, but that's a given. We're always doing something wrong or — better

This move needs to be played well by you if you plan on moving forward with her. Played wrong it will appear cliché and look like you're trying too hard.

yet — something not right, the way she wants it done. Once you convince her it's just your idea for the two of you to have a good time, she's going to light up.)

Think of it this way for a moment: You're lying in a park, nibblin' on cheese, sippin' wine, avoiding the chores list at home, and she thinks this is the best thing you've done for her in months. Seems like a no-brainer, doesn't it? She is always fondest when you consider her needs over yours. So take advantage and enjoy. I no longer look at the picnic as a romantic challenge but as a great way to spend an afternoon, no doubt increasing your odds of some "romance" to follow.

This presents an opportunity to show off a culinary side she will enjoy. If it's done on impulse, a fresh loaf of sourdough, a ripe avocado, a chunk of Brie and a chilled bottle of Pinot Grigio is an undeniable combination. For a planned afternoon in the park, we need to provide a little more substance.

With a little preparation there is no reason the two of you have to settle for cold deli sandwiches instead of a warm meal away from the house. For the soup, I recommend you warm the crab at home and place it in a container that will retain the heat. And prepare the chicken sandwiches at home and wrap in foil to keep warm until you get to your destination.

To me...cooking is the same as sex.
You put your heart, your passion,
and love in to your food in order to
get an orgasmic finish.

— George Kyrtatas, America's Little Greek Chef

PICNIC BAGUETTE

INGREDIENTS

Fresh baguettes 2

Brie . . . . .2 oz.

Avocado . . . . .1 medium

Roma tomatoes . . . . .2 small

Basil . . . . 4 sprigs

Butter .2 tablespoons

Step one

- Cut baguettes lengthwise.
- Slice Brie, tomato and avocado. Separate basil leaves from stems.

Step two

- Lightly butter one side of each baguette.
- Add a layer of basil, Brie, tomato and avocado. Replace top half.

Step three

- Slice and serve.

CHILLED CANTALOUPE SOUP WITH WARM CRAB

INGREDIENTS

Shallot 1

Lime 1

Crabmeat . . . . .2 oz.

Cantaloupe . . . . 2 cups

Olive oil . . . . .1 tablespoon

Dijon mustard . . . . .½ teaspoon

Sugar . . . . .1 tablespoon

Half and half or cream . . . . .2 tablespoons

Salt and pepper . . . . to taste

Step one

- Mince 1 tablespoon of shallot and squeeze 1 tablespoon of lime juice.
- Chop crabmeat into ½-inch squares.
- Cut cantaloupe into ¾-inch squares.

Step two

- Heat olive oil in small pan over medium heat.
- Add minced shallot and cook for 1 minute.
- Add lime juice and mustard and stir.
- Add crabmeat and cook for 2 minutes.
- Remove from heat and set aside.

Step three

- Bring 2 tablespoons water to the boil in a small saucepan.
- Add sugar to create simple syrup.

Step four

- Transfer syrup, cantaloupe and half and half to blender and puree.
- Season with salt and pepper.

Step five

- Mound crab in center of two bowls.
- Pour the soup around the crab and serve.

Serves 2

CHICKEN CHUTNEY BURGERS

INGREDIENTS

Arugula . . . . 2-3 oz.

Ciabatta rolls 4

Boneless, skinless chicken thighs . . . . . . 1lb.

Mango or other chutney . . . . 1 small jar

Swiss cheese . . . . 4 slices

Red onion . . . . ½ small

Avocado 1

Tip
Any chutney will
work...mango is
most common.

Step one
- Slice onions and avocado
- Remove arugula leaves from stems.
- Slice rolls crosswise.

Step two
- Preheat grill on medium heat.
- Add chicken thighs and cook until done, approximately 10 minutes.

Step three
- While thighs are cooking, toast or broil inner surfaces of rolls.

Step four
- Assemble sandwiches, placing a chicken thigh and a small amount of chutney on one side of each bun.
- Add cheese, arugula, onion and avocado on the other side.

Serves 4

Her Dinner Party

There is a defining moment in life when a man who is courting a woman loses his identity. He becomes half of a couple.

No longer do plans and events revolve around his desires, but around that of the couple. Gone is the "What are you up to?" question, replaced by "What are the two of you doing?" It's a new stage in life when you realize that you have to participate in and put on events that cater to a specific crowd — your couple friends.

And for couples, the dinner party is a winner. It is a prime opportunity to get your friends together all at once and tends to be less costly than gathering at a local restaurant and typically more memorable.

If you're still single, you still get invited to such gatherings and are encouraged to bring a date. It appears to be a perfect setting to meet your friends. Beware! Couples think it is their purpose to play matchmaker with their single friends.

The curiosity of the others mounts as you arrive.

The ladies will gather: "Who is she? Where did they meet? She's thin."

The guys will gather: "Who's that? How did he score her? Nice tits!"

And the party begins.

Within the next 5 to 30 minutes, the following conversation will inevitably take place:

"Where did you two meet?"

"That's so great!"

"How long have you been dating?"

"You make such a great couple."

"Are you thinking about getting married?"

That fast. It strikes that fast.

Talk about a momentum shift. Your carefree and sometimes silly behavior that originally attracted her is forgotten, and you now find yourself fending off the "Where is this relationship going?" question.

Thus the moral of this interlude into the dinner party is if single, you might want to show up solo. There will be plenty of parties to attend with a steady date later.

Dinner parties usually require ample cooking time, and there's a good chance that the two of you will work on the meal together. By now, you have hopefully developed an appreciation for the peace and harmony that coexist with cooking in the kitchen — especially if you have an ESPN feed coming in over the fridge.

Among the differences between men and women are details. Women can spend years mapping out every detail of a wedding, while we simply ask, "Is it open-bar?"

Guys will concentrate on the food but often overlook the other details. Don't worry; she won't. Among the differences between men and women are details. Women can spend years mapping out every detail of a wedding, while we simply ask, "Is it open-bar?" knowing that the answer to that question will determine whether it's a good or bad wedding.

She will handle most of the decorative details of the evening, which of course cannot be accomplished without a few new purchases for the house. Her eye for decorative detail goes hand in hand with her joy of shopping.

You have to concentrate on the meal. There is a lot involved in preparing her dinner party and there are moments when the two of you can have a lot of fun working together in the kitchen during the preparation. But the key to her party's success is your ability to handle the kitchen efforts, freeing her to host your guests. If you can successfully dazzle the group with the food while she keeps her hands clean, she just might be pushing them out the door after that last glass of wine, and — well, hopefully you've got the idea by now.

Don't attempt to wing this on the day-of with a "We'll see if this works" attitude. Women are very competitive and don't accept failure. I also was competitive when I was young. Then I became a teenager and decided that I liked women. I learned to accept failure ever since. Not on this occasion.

A successful day starts with organization. I have provided you with a five-course menu for the evening, with tips on what you can prepare in advance.

Get the cleanup out of the way early. That's the part of the preparation that stresses her out, and if she is stressed out, the kitchen starts to get touchy. So get the cleaning done and the table set. This will allow the two of you to enjoy the pleasures of the cooking preparation.

Next, establish the sporting event on the tube, tune the volume low and get the Gordon Lightfoot cranked — if not Lightfoot, some soothing music that you both enjoy. It's relaxing.

The stresses of hosting a party push many couples to the edge. They shouldn't. If you're organized, you should be able to have fun with it. Get the shopping done in advance, but inevitably you're going to forget something. Working together, one of you can make the run to the store while the other holds the course in the kitchen.

And remember to invite the appropriate number of guests for your dining room. I've set the menu for eight (or four couples), which most dining rooms can handle.

If all of this appears to be overwhelming and not worth it, remember this: If you recall from Her Bunco Night Potluck in Book One, third-party endorsement is much stronger than self-promotion. Women consider their guys schmucks until someone else reminds them of what a catch you are. It'll come back at a later date what great parties you throw and what a talented guy she has. You play to win the season, not the game.

Author's Hope
Don't bank on it, but if you are truly organized and she is aware of the surefire success of the evening, there might be a time for a quickie prior to guest arrival. Albeit doubtful, it's lofty goals like this that keep us trying.

HER DINNER PARTY MENU

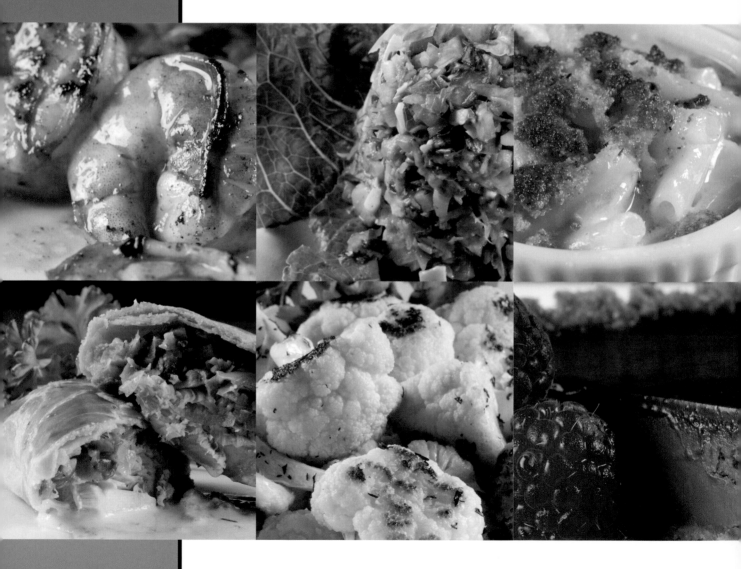

Hors d'oeuvres

Spicy Shrimp Skewers
Soy-Lime marinated pan seared shrimp

Salad

Chopped Salad
*Finely chopped vegetables, chicken and blue cheese
combined for enhanced flavor and presentation*

Pasta

Crab Mac & Cheese
Guyere and white cheddar macaroni with dungenous crab

Main Course

Salmon Wellington
*Pastry encrusted filet of salmon with mushroom artichoke stuffing
served with a lemon dill cream sauce*

Vegetable

Roasted Cauliflower Florets
Oven roasted cauliflower tossed in fresh thyme

Dessert

Chocolate Tart
Graham cracker crusted chocolate tart served with fresh berries

SPICY SHRIMP SKEWERS

Shrimp is enjoyed by most, thus this is a high-probability play at a dinner party.

INGREDIENTS

Raw shrimp, peeled and deveined . . . . . .2 lbs.

Special Equipment:

Large toothpicks or skewers

Marinade:

Lime . . . . .1, juiced

Worcestershire sauce . . . . 2 tablespoons

Soy sauce . . . . 2 tablespoons

Olive oil . . . . 2 tablespoons

Cayenne pepper . . . . ½ teaspoon

Step one

• Skewer shrimp, one to two per skewer.

Step two

• Mix remaining ingredients to make marinade.

• Marinate skewered shrimp for 15 minutes.

Step three

• Preheat a large pan and cook shrimp, about 1 minute per side, over medium-high heat.

• Place on tray and serve.

Serves 8-10

CHOPPED SALAD

Finely chopping all of the ingredients allows all of the flavors to blend in every bite and eliminates the need for excessive dressing.

100

INGREDIENTS

Tomatoes	2
Avocado	1
Red onion	1
Celery	1 stalk
Parsley	1 bunch
Hard-boiled eggs whites	12
Blue cheese	4 oz.
Boneless, skinless chicken breast	1
Iceberg lettuce	1 head
Romaine lettuce	1 head
White wine vinegar	1 tablespoon
Olive oil	2½ tablespoons
Salt and pepper	to taste

Step one
- Heat 1 teaspoon olive oil in small pan.
- Add chicken breast and cook over low heat until done, approximately 10 minutes.

Step two
- Chop all solid ingredients to the same size, ¼-inch or smaller.

Step three
- Transfer approximately equal portions (about 1 cup each) of tomato, avocado, onion, celery, parsley, egg whites, cheese and chicken with two equal portions (about 2 cups each) of iceberg and romaine to a bowl.

Step four
- In a small cup, mix remaining 2 tablespoons olive oil and vinegar.

Step five
- Toss all ingredients and add salt and pepper to taste.

Step six
- For individual servings, pack salad into cup and turn over onto plate.

Serves 8

CRAB MAC & CHEESE

INGREDIENTS

Mixture:

Pasta or macaroni . . . . 10 oz.

Butter . . . . 3 tablespoons

Flour . . . . 3 tablespoons

Milk . . . . 2 ¾ cups

Salt and pepper . . . . .to taste

Gruyere cheese . . . . 2 oz.

White cheddar . . . . 4 oz., grated

Dungeness or blue crab . . . . 8 oz.

Toppings:

Fine dry bread crumbs . . . . 4 tablespoons

Butter . . . . 2 tablespoons

Step one

- Preheat oven to 375 degrees.
- Bring large pot of water to boil with 1 tablespoon of salt.
- Add pasta and cook for approximately 8 to 10 minutes (do not overcook).

Step two

- Melt butter in medium saucepan over medium heat.
- Add flour and whisk until smooth.
- Continue stirring while slowly adding 2¼ cups milk; whisk until smooth.

Step three

- Season with salt and pepper.
- Gradually add cheeses and stir until smooth. Fold in crab.

Step four

- Transfer mixture to large bowl and gently fold in cooked pasta.
- Line up eight ramekins and put 1 tablespoon of milk in each.
- Pour in filling evenly.

Step five

- Combine bread crumbs and melted butter
- Sprinkle evenly over ramekins.

Step six

- Bake until golden brown and bubbling around the edges, approximately 15 to 20 minutes.

Serves 8

SALMON WELLINGTONS

INGREDIENTS

Salmon fillets . . . . 8, about ¾ inch thick

Filling:

Butter . . . . 3 tablespoons

Shallots. . . . . .1 cup minced

Artichoke buttons . . . . .1 cup minced

Mushrooms. . . . . .2 cups minced

Salt and pepper. . . . . .to taste

Pastry:

Butter . . . . ½ pound, at room temperature

Cream cheese . . . . 8 oz., at room temperature

Flour. . . . . 2 cups

Egg yolk 1

Milk or half and half . . . . 1 tablespoon

Sauce:

Butter . . . . 1 tablespoon

Shallots or onions. 3 tablespoons minced

Flour. . . . . 1 tablespoon

Lemon . . . . .1 small

Fresh dill. . . . . 4 tablespoons

Half and half. . . . . .1½ cups

Step one

Filling

- Melt butter in large pan over medium heat.
- Add shallots and artichokes and cook for 2 minutes.
- Add mushrooms and cook until mushrooms are soft, 4 to 5 minutes, stirring constantly.
- Salt and pepper to taste.
- Remove from heat and let cool.

Step two

Prepare Pastry

- Mix butter and cream cheese in a bowl until well blended.
- Add flour and continue mixing until well incorporated.
- Shape into two flat balls and refrigerate for several hours, or overnight.

Step three

Prepare Pastry , Next Step

- Roll half of pastry on a floured board into a rectangle approximately 14 inches by 12 inches.
- Cut into four rectangles and repeat with remaining dough.

Step four

- Place salmon fillets on a greased baking sheet.
- Tuck thinner parts of fillets underneath, making them all the same thickness.
- Divide filling among the fillets and spread evenly on top.

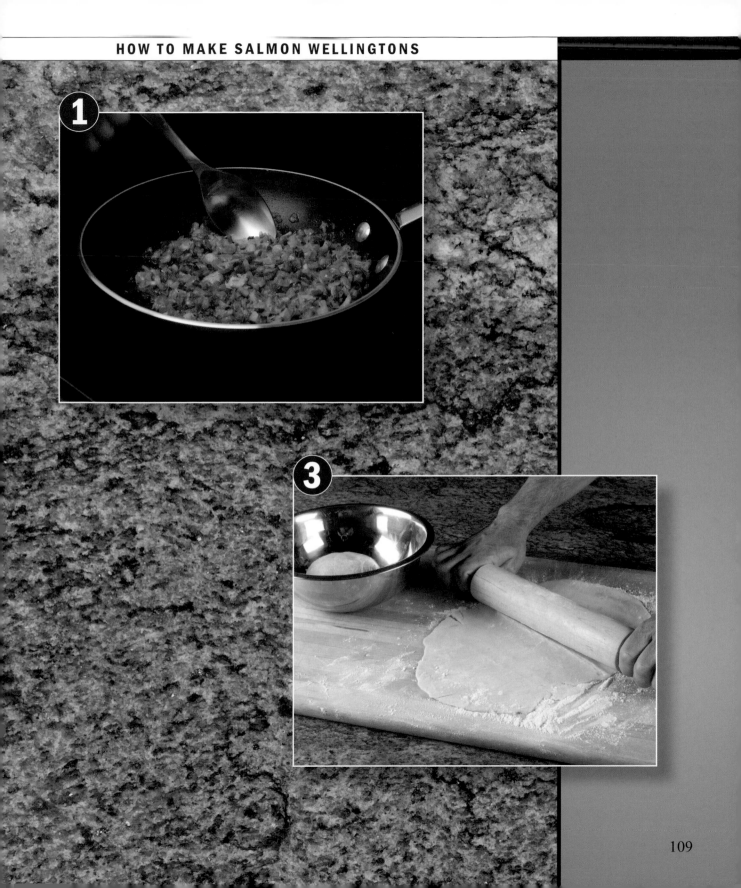

Step five

- Cover each Wellington with a rectangle of pastry.
- Tuck ½ inch of pastry under fillets and trim off excess dough. (Do not cover the entire bottom with pastry, or it will become soggy.)

Step six

- Mix egg yolk and 1 tablespoon of milk.
- Brush top and sides of Wellingtons with glaze, being careful not to let glaze drip.

Step seven

- If Wellingtons have been refrigerated, bring them to room temperature, approximately 1 hour.
- Preheat oven to 425 degrees. Bake Wellingtons for 20 to 25 minutes, or until pastry is golden. (At this time, if the fillets are ¾ inch thick, they will be moist and flaky.)

Step eight

- While Wellingtons are baking, prepare sauce.
- Melt 1 tablespoon of butter in a small pan.
- Add shallots or onions and cook over medium heat for two minutes.
- Add flour and stir.
- Add juice of lemon.
- Slowly add half and half and fresh dill.

Step nine

- Spoon a small amount of sauce on each plate.
- Place Wellingtons on sauce and put remaining sauce in serving dish.

Serves 8

Tip

You can re-roll scraps of pastry and cut out small decorations; place on Wellingtons and glaze entire pastries again. Individual Wellingtons can be refrigerated up to 8 hours.

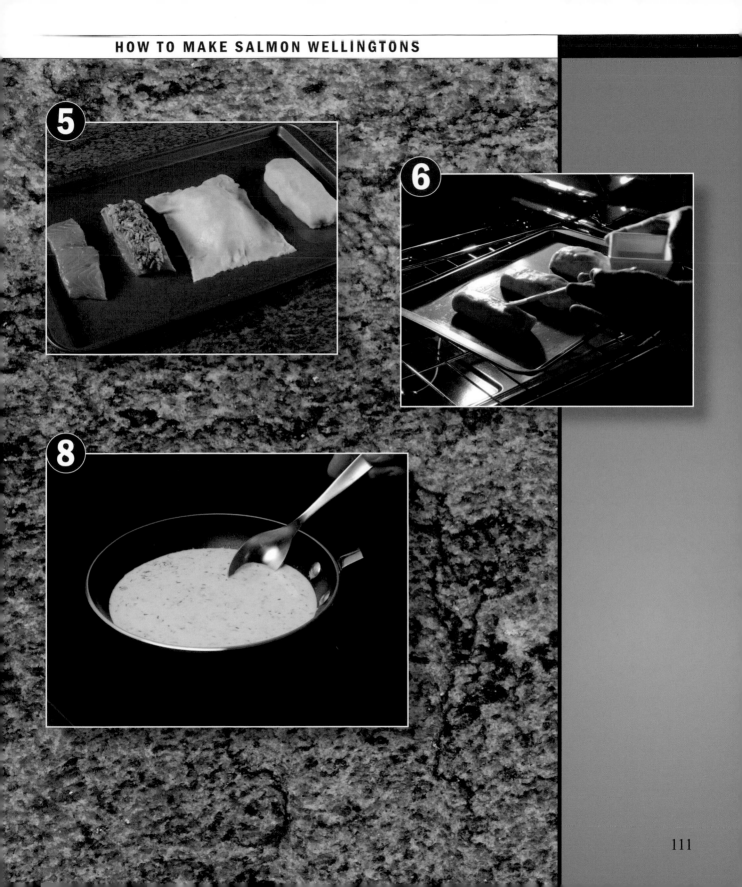

ROASTED CAULIFLOWER FLORETS

INGREDIENTS

Cauliflower . . . . 2 heads
Fresh thyme. . . . . .1 bunch
Olive oil . . . . .3 tablespoons
Salt . . . . 2 teaspoons

Step one

• Preheat oven to 400 degrees.

Step two

• Break cauliflower heads into florets.

• Remove thyme leaves from stems.

Step three

• Combine florets and olive oil in large bowl and toss to coat.

• Add salt and 2 tablespoons of thyme and toss again.

Step four

• Place florets on cookie sheet.

Step five

• Roast for 45 minutes, or until golden brown.

Step six

• Plate for presentation.

Serves 8

His Dinner Party:
the Cookout

When it's our turn to host a party, we lean toward the cookout. Gone are the formalities of elegant table settings, folded napkins, tucked-in shirts and closed-toed shoes.

It's time for shorts, T-shirts, beer and wine straight from the cooler and a bevy of eats that you can pile high on your plate. This is a casual affair that you serve yourself, more than once.

There's something about hanging out by the grill that brings forth a casual atmosphere of moving around the patio, drinking, eating and socializing. These parties are at their best with a variety of dishes that allow you to graze all afternoon while bouncing from person to person.

I recommend that when you host a group gathering, you design the courses with mobility in mind and let your guests find their own seats. This creates movement throughout the meal and allows people to sit in more than one place or just lean on a counter nibbling while enjoying conversation. It is this casual atmosphere that makes a summer cookout social and unpretentious.

Now wait! I am not suggesting a bunch of spare ribs being devoured with one hand while the sauce is washed down with a cold one from the keg in the other. Guys can be guilty of taking casual to the extreme. I have been to many stag barbeques where the paper plates were left untouched as we ate straight from the grill and wiped our hands on our jeans. As long as there were sufficient provisions of beer in the cooler, ribs and chicken on the grill and some chips as an appetizer, all was good. Don't get me wrong; I am not one to ever turn down such an affair, but be that we are talking about more than just a tailgate party and the guests are aware of our new-found cooking talents, we are looking to upgrade our spread worthy of everyone's approval. A couple's life is full of compromise. Together, the cookout will need a little upgrade.

She will be happy to focus her energy on the décor.

"Do the plates match the napkins?"

"Should the table be on that side of the patio?"

"Do you like these glasses?"

"Is my outfit OK?"

It never stops.

When hosting a co-ed cookout, you need to establish some common ground, a plan that balances the consumption necessities we need with the elements of décor that increase the probability of getting her in the mood.

> **Note**
> *Most guys have only two concerns when arriving at a cookout: "What are you grillin?" and "Where's the cooler?"*

Guys can be guilty of taking casual to the extreme.

Let's start with the set-up. There is nothing wrong with a couple of floral arrangements; women enjoy them. Just stick with the primary hues on the color wheel and save pinks and purples for her baby and bridal showers.

I like to provide sufficient small plates and bowls to allow for mobility and let guests feel free to make continuous attacks on the spread. Ceramic is nice. If going paper, get the good stuff to allow for the potential pile-up. The plate has to be able to hold up with two fingers below and the thumb on the top rim.

Men want to grill. Every guy I know appreciates the grill, and most would consider grilling as their contribution to the household cooking. It is assumed that men know how to grill, yet alarmingly, most don't. Pouring one's Budweiser on the coals to drown the flames that are burning the steaks does not create flavor, and you can grill without a need for sauces and rubs. Remember, ingredients,

ingredients and ingredients. Good cuts of meat can stand on their own with the proper grilling attention.

This is not the only element of the meal, but since the term "cookout" is derived from the concept of cooking outside of the house, we are generally talking about grilling. A quality cookout cannot survive on the grill alone and succeeds on the supplementary dishes, but most guests will be expecting something to be charbroiled.

There is one common mistake that many men make when grilling. Either from a general lack of patience or an effort to show that they are working hard at the 'que, many make the mistake of playing too much with the meat. Leave it alone and let the grill do the work. It is a heat source much like an oven. The only trick is to know where the hot spots are so you can manage all of the cuts cooking evenly.

Quality side dishes will make the cookout memorable. A good cookout does in fact require some cooking from the kitchen. For most of the country, cookouts are limited to the warm seasons from late spring to early fall and the general idea is celebrating the weather by eating outside. The dishes should be compatible to such fare.

Cookouts tend to start earlier, while the sun is still shining, so the cocktails should remain on the lighter side. Hold the whiskeys for later in the evening. Wine, as always, is going to please, especially if the wine is good. I prefer the host to use the good stuff on me and so do your guests. Have plenty on hand.

Wine, as always, is going to please, especially if the wine is good. I prefer the host to use the good stuff on me and so do your guests. Have plenty on hand.

CREAMED LAMB QUESADILLAS

INGREDIENTS

Tomato	1 medium
Cilantro	6 sprigs
Jalapeno pepper	1
Salt and pepper	to taste
Tomatillo	1
Brie	8 oz.
Avocados	2 medium
Lamb leg	1 pound
Onion	1 small
Olive oil	2 tablespoon
Flour	1 tablespoon
Sour cream	¼ cup
8-inch flour tortillas	16

Step one

Prepare salsa

- Mince tomato, cilantro, jalapeno and tomatillo.
- Mix in small bowl, add salt and pepper and set aside.

Step two

- Cut Brie and avocados into ¼-inch slices.
- Cut lamb into ½-inch squares.
- Cut onion into ¼-inch squares.

Step three

- Heat olive oil in large pan over medium heat.
- Add lamb and onions to pan and cook until done, approximately 5 minutes.

Step four

- Sprinkle with flour and stir for 30 seconds.
- Add sour cream and stir until warm, about 1 minute.
- Add salsa, stir and remove from heat.

Step five

- Preheat grill or large pan to medium heat.
- Place Brie sparingly on one flour tortilla and sliced avocado on second tortilla.
- Add about 2 tablespoons of lamb-salsa mixture on top of avocado.
- Top with the Brie tortilla.
- Repeat step until eight quesadillas are prepared.

Step six

- Grill and cook until cheese is melted, 1 to 2 minutes on each side.

Step seven

- Cut and serve.

Serves 8

LEFT COAST SALAD

Los Angeles is often referred to as the land of fruits and nuts — but not because of this dish. Combining the two makes a great tasty salad.

INGREDIENTS

Mixed greens	12 ounces
Raspberries	1 cup
Blueberries	1 cup
Blackberries	1 cup
Cantaloupe	1 cup
Honeydew	1 cup
Goat cheese	4 oz. (½ cup)
Chopped walnuts	4 oz. (½ cup)

Lemon Vinaigrette:

Olive oil	3 tablespoons
Lemon juice	2 tablespoons
White wine vinegar	1 tablespoon

Step one

- Cut cantaloupe and honeydew melon into ½ squares.
- Crumble goat cheese.

Step two

Prepare lemon vinaigrette:

- Mix oil, lemon juice and vinegar in a small cup.

Step three

- Combine all remaining ingredients in a large salad bowl.
- Add lemon vinaigrette.
- Toss and serve.

Serves 8

ROASTED PIG

This is a great party offering. Pork rump and/or shoulder is relatively inexpensive yet flavorful, so you won't have to spend your entire paycheck entertaining friends (or you will at least have more money to spend on the essentials — booze, beer and wine).

INGREDIENTS

Pork rump roast	3 pounds
Cilantro	12 sprigs
Sour cream	1 cup
Milk	¼ cup
Horseradish	2 tablespoons

Step one

- Cut pork into approximately 2½-inch pieces.
- Heat grill to high.

Step two

- Grill until pork is done, 25 to 30 minutes.

Step three

- While pig is cooking, make sauce.
- Place cilantro and sour cream in a blender.
- Add milk as needed to assist blending.
- Blend until cilantro is finely minced.
- Transfer to a small bowl and add horseradish.

Step four

- Remove pork from grill and place on plates.
- Serve with sauce.

Serves 8

Tip
Pig also can be cooked in the oven in a large roasting pan at 475 degrees for about 40 minutes.

LAYERED EGGPLANT

INGREDIENTS

Eggplant . . . . 2 large

Tomatoes . . . . 2 large

Yellow or summer squash . . . . 2 large

Onion . . . . 1 medium

Spinach . . . . 1 bunch

Olive oil . . . . 2 tablespoons

Goat cheese . . . . 3 oz.

Shredded cheddar cheese . . . . 3 oz.

Salt and pepper . . . . to taste

Step one

- Peel eggplant and cut into ¼-inch slices.
- Cut tomatoes into ½-inch squares.
- Cut squash into ⅛-inch slices.
- Mince onions and crumble goat cheese.
- Remove stems from spinach and cut leaves crosswise into ¾-inch strips.

Step two

- Preheat 1 tablespoon of olive oil in large pan over medium heat.
- Add spinach and cook for approximately 2 minutes.
- Remove from heat and let cool.

Step three

- Rub remaining olive oil in 9-by-13-inch baking dish.
- Arrange a layer of eggplant on bottom of dish, followed by a layer of tomatoes (salt and pepper lightly) and a layer of squash.
- Sprinkle with onions.
- Add a layer of eggplant followed by a layer of spinach.
- Sprinkle with goat cheese.
- Add a layer of eggplant, followed by a layer of tomatoes (salt and pepper lightly) and a layer of squash.
- Sprinkle with onions.
- Add layer of eggplant and cover with cheddar cheese.

Step four

- Preheat oven to 400 degrees.
- Cover dish with aluminum foil and bake for 45 minutes.
- Remove foil and bake until tender, approximately 15 additional minutes

Variation

Other items like mushrooms, different squashes and different cheeses are great. Be creative and experiment.

Serves 8

SWEET POTS AND YAMS

INGREDIENTS

Yams 3

Sweet potatoes 3

Olive oil . . . . 2 tablespoons

Maple syrup . . . . 3 tablespoons

Step one

- Preheat oven to 400 degrees.
- Peel yams and sweet potatoes.
- Cut in erratic shapes, approximately the same size.

Step two

- Combine yams and potatoes and olive oil in large bowl and toss to coat.

Step three

- Place on cookie sheet.
- Bake for approximately 30 minutes.

Step four

- Remove from oven.
- Drizzle with maple syrup.
- Return to oven until done, approximately 10 minutes.

Serves 8

The Casual Dress
Friday Potluck

I think the best reason to encourage your kid to get an education is that he has a chance to work in an office— with a lot of women.

He gets to work in an air-conditioned, well-furnished space, not in a solemn warehouse or outdoors in the dead heat of summer. It's a place where you wear sharp suits, shave, comb your hair and rarely break a sweat. For most guys, work is the only time we look good all week, and also why we don't dress up for our cookouts.

Looking good by dressing sharp does take its toll on the workforce, which is why some innovative human-resource manager came up with the Casual Dress Friday. It's not every Friday, but with most companies one Friday a month, on which you are allowed to let your hair down, so to speak.

Actually, you can't do that. There are many restrictions on dressing casually at the office. You still have to shave, comb your hair and wear a collared shirt that is tucked into a clean pair of casual slacks. And the ladies still have to do their makeup and hair and dress appropriately for the office. So "casual" is a relative term. Dare anyone to see what I look like on a true casual Friday working from home.

But with Casual Dress Friday comes the Casual Friday Potluck. It's a chance for the staff to stay in for lunch, gather around some food and socialize and get to know their colleagues better. This is the essence of the casual day. It's a morale-booster and a chance to develop a more relaxed environment among the staff to increase productivity. Most of the offices that I've passed through appear pretty relaxed already and the staff finds a way to spend plenty of time socializing (and gossiping, for that matter). But if the company encourages a Casual Dress Friday Potluck, your best move is to partake.

Where better to display your culinary talents than to all of your colleagues at work? Not in an effort to court one of the ladies in the office, but to show off your skills to co-workers and your bosses. If you're single, co-workers have single friends. If you're not, your motive is to impress your bosses. Bosses have decision-making power on promotion opportunities, and they're looking for well-rounded individuals to promote. Promotions lead to pay raises. Pay raises lead to attractiveness.

The Potluck is one of those opportunities. There are others, such as volunteering your weekend time helping with a community-affairs activity that the company has sponsored, but let's compare the two. One opportunity to impress your boss takes place during your valuable weekend; the other takes place during the workweek. End of comparison.

Promotions lead to pay raises. Pay raises lead to attractiveness.

You have a total advantage going in. I rarely recall any guys taking the initiative to bring something other than a tray of cheese cubes that they grabbed at the grocery store on the way to the office. I can't score at home with cheese cubes; I'm definitely not going to make points at work. Store-bought dishes are never talked about later. He who brings the good stuff is. This can't hurt your image with the higher-ups.

Let's face it; if you have a special someone at home who is enamored by the culinary abilities you acquired from *Will Cook for Sex*, she is still a human, and we are a material bunch. The cooking will definitely enhance those special evenings and she does brag about you to her friends, but everyone can't help but gauge their happiness by the almighty dollar. That little extra in your Friday paycheck can be very attractive.

So we take our efforts to the office to impress our colleagues and management in hopes of a remembrance when promotion time rolls around.

Happy Hour
Side Note

Happy hour side note: If a promotion is not what you're after, don't forget that Casual Dress Friday usually ends with Happy Hour Margaritas at the local watering hole after work. If you're looking for a leg up with the ladies in the office, it's nice to have them raving about your cooking skills that they tasted earlier that day. The Happy Hour Margarita is the true aphrodisiac. Oysters on the half shell and/or fried shrimp eyes at the sushi bar are merely tales created by the proprietors of these establishments to laugh at us silly fools who buy into this crap and beg our women to eat them. Most women get sick rather than sexual.

That's not the case with the Happy Hour Margarita. There is something special about that citrus cocktail that so puts her in the mood.

These are my arguments for the importance of the Casual Dress Friday Potluck.

I can't score at home with cheese cubes; I'm definitely not going to make points at work.

Until I met Rocky Fino several years ago, I seldom did more than grill an occasional steak or fish. He took the fear out of it and showed me that anyone can do a respectable job. Now I cook with beer. Sometimes I even add it to the food.

— Gary Monterosso, Beer columnist
Host of *Still Crazy After All These Beers*

LAMB POPS

If you step up to the plate with this offering at a company potluck, your bosses will take notice.

INGREDIENTS

Rack of lamb 3

Mint . . . . .1 bunch

Sour cream . . . . 1 cup

Milk . . . . ¼ cup

Horseradish . . . . .2 tablespoons

Salt and pepper . . . . to taste

Step one

- Trim fat and membranes from lamb.
- Coarsely chop mint, saving a few sprigs for garnish.

Step two

- Cut lamb racks into individual chops.
- Lightly salt and pepper chops on both sides.

Step three

Prepare dipping sauce

- Place mint and sour cream in blender and blend until mint is finely minced, adding milk as needed to assist blending.
- Transfer to small bowl and add horseradish.

Step four

- Preheat grill on high.
- Place chops on grill and cook 2 to 3 minutes per side.

Step five

- Serve with dipping sauce.

Serves 8-10

FINGERLING CANAPES

INGREDIENTS

Fingerling potatoes. 12

Fresh dill . . . . 4 sprigs

Olive oil . . . . 1½ tablespoons

Salt and pepper . . . . to taste

Sour cream . . . . ½ cup

Lumpfish caviar . . . . 2 ounces

Tip
For dollops, place sour cream in a plastic sandwich bag, snip the corner and gently squeeze onto potatoes.

Step one

- Preheat oven to 400 degrees.
- Halve potatoes lengthwise.
- Mince dill.

Step two

- Toss potatoes in olive oil.
- Lightly salt and pepper.
- Place on cookie sheet, cut side down.

Step three

- Bake in oven until tender and brown on bottom, 25 to 30 minutes.
- Remove from oven and let cool.

Step four

- Transfer potatoes to serving tray, cut side up.
- Dollop each with sour cream and top with caviar.
- Sprinkle with dill and serve.

Note

Better caviar, better dish: If you have the means, use beluga.

Serves 10-12

HOT SHOT SALAD

INGREDIENTS

Watercress . . . . 3 bunches

Mache or mesclun greens . . . . 4 oz.

Pomegranate 1

Oranges . . . . 2 medium

Feta cheese. . . . . 4 ounces

Sliced almonds . . . . 4 ounces

Jalapeno Vinaigrette:

Olive oil . . . . ¼ cup

Jalapeno pepper 1

White wine vinegar . . . . 2 tablespoons

Step one

- Chop watercress and greens into ¾-inch lengths.
- Remove seeds from pomegranate.
- Remove seeds and finely mince jalapeno.
- Peel oranges, remove white pith and cut into ½-inch dice.
- Crumble feta.

Step two

Prepare jalapeno vinaigrette

- Mix oil, vinegar and jalapeno in a small bowl.

Step three

- Preheat oven to 400 degrees.
- Place almonds on cookie sheet and toast for approximately 5 minutes.

Step four

- Combine all ingredients except vinaigrette in a large bowl.
- Add vinaigrette and toss.

Serves 8 – 10

HEARTLAND GUMBO

By no means a true New Orleans-style gumbo, but a simpler, milder, similar rendition to get you started.

INGREDIENTS

Raw chicken	1½ pounds (4 cups)
Italian sausage	1 lb.
Raw shrimp, peeled and deveined	1 lb.
Onion	1 medium
Pasilla pepper	1
Tomatoes	2 medium
Celery	2 stalks
Flour	1 tablespoon
Cayenne pepper	½ teaspoon
Chicken broth	5 cups
Milk	½ cup
Salt and pepper	to taste

Step one

- Cut chicken, sausage and shrimp into ½-inch cubes.
- Cut onion, pepper, tomatoes and celery into ½-inch cubes.

Step two

- Heat olive oil in large pot.
- Add chicken, sausage and shrimp and cook for approximately 5 minutes.
- Sprinkle with flour and stir.

Step three

- Add remaining ingredients except milk and simmer for 30 minutes.

Step four

- Add milk.
- Add salt and pepper to taste and serve hot.

Serves 10

FRENCH DIP LAMB

Every city has a famous eatery that has survived the test of time and maintained the style and feel from generations past. Growing up in Los Angeles, Philippe's is that eatery. They are legendary for their French-dip sandwiches, served with one of the best hot mustards you will ever find, and they have added a decent wine list in recent years that is quite the surprise for a place that still has sawdust on the floor.

INGREDIENTS

Whole leg of lamb 1

French rolls or baguettes . . 12 sliced in half

Swiss cheese . . . . 12 slices

Hot mustard . . . . 1 jar

Beef stock . . . . 1 quart

Step one

- Preheat oven to 275 degrees.
- Place lamb in broiling pan and cover with aluminum foil.
- Roast until done, approximately three hours.

Step two

- Transfer lamb to platter and set aside.

Step three

- Remove drippings from roasting pan, skimming off grease, and put in medium saucepan.
- Add beef stock and bring to boil.
- Transfer to flat bowl for dipping.

Step four

- Slice lamb cross-wise from leg.
- Add desired portion to bottom half of each roll.
- Add slice of cheese and mustard to taste.
- Dip top half of roll (or both halves, if preferred) in sauce.

Step five

- Close sandwich and serve.

Variation

Swiss cheese can be substituted with other white cheeses.

Serves 12

The Little League Team Party

Sex after children? It can happen. Not often, not easy and not for long.

Kids have an uncanny sixth sense about their parents' libidos — that, or they're eavesdropping when she leans in and says, "Honey, I'm horny." Because no matter what you do to distract them with television, video games, ice-cream bars, etc., they find a way to pound on that locked door before you can get your jeans off. Strategies vary from house to house — and are developed over time — on how to manage a sex life between the constant barrage of "I want …", "Can I have …?" and "Mommy, he's pulling my hair …"

Kids are a drain.

Once you have them, romance is much more difficult. Sex is more of a rarity (which is why romance is more difficult on us guys, because we put on our romance caps for the sake of having sex).

Life transitions from us — to them. The social calendar revolves around the kids' extracurricular activities, which we sit through with a smile, no matter how bad the team plays. Add to that their undeveloped taste buds and any time spent with kids usually limits the gourmet possibilities. The combination of our kids determining what they will eat and too much reliability on pre-packaged food has made any event involving children consist of hot dogs, chips and delivery pizza.

That wasn't the case when I was growing up. The end-of-the-season team party was an opportunity for the players and parents alike to have some fun. The party was hosted by the coach or team mom at their residence, not Chuck E. Cheese, and some good food was prepared with both in mind.

When we hosted the party at our house, my old man took over in the kitchen. I can't tell you if he ever got his just rewards for hosting the team parties; like many of you, I don't care to consider such activities by my parents. But those parties

> **Add children and all of their demands to the mix and romance is found through her novels and your nudie mags.**

are still talked about in some of the old Little League circles, for they were more memorable than the old pizza parlor parties.

Married-with-children changes the playing field. It's difficult enough to keep the spice in a long-term relationship, such as a marriage. Add children and all of their demands to the mix and romance is found through her novels and your nudie mags.

But one thing does not change in this world, and that's women comparing the value of their men with that of their friends' men. Which brings us full-circle back to the reason we would host such an event.

I've pulled a couple of ageless recipes from the days of my old man hosting the parties and added our own pizza recipe, which you can make with the kids. Your topping options are endless, the kids are thrilled to make their own creations and the moms love nothing more than seeing you interact with the kids.

It's a win-win situation. She gets turned on seeing you having fun in the kitchen making pizzas with the kids, which once again opens the window of opportunity for a potential score once the kids crash later that evening.

I apologize for the redundancy, but I'm one-dimensional when it comes to motivation.

NOTE
At first glance, this section would appear to fall into the category of a couples-only event. Take a closer look and you will find plenty of single moms and dads in the youth-athletics bleachers.

Rocky has a great passion for food and with his witty humor and love shows us how we can connect with other people over a great meal. Whether you are trying to impress a hot date or feed a family of four, this book is a must have in any kitchen.

— Jewels and Jill Elmore,
Private Chefs and Authors of The Family Chef

149

TEAM SALAD

Aside from potato salad, kids tend to avoid most salads. This is not the healthiest choice, but they will like it and it's a start.

INGREDIENTS

Bacon . . . . 8 strips

Iceberg lettuce . . . . 2 heads

Red or green seedless grapes 24

Tomatoes . . . . 2 large

Sunflower seeds . . . . 4 ounces

Dressing:

Mayonnaise . . . . ½ cup

Ketchup . . . . 2 tablespoons

Step one

- Heat a large pan over medium heat.
- Cook bacon until well done, turning occasionally.
- Set aside on paper towels.

Step two

- Cut lettuce into ¾-inch squares.
- Cut grapes in half (or quarters, if large).
- Cut bacon and tomatoes into 1/2-inch squares.

Step three

Prepare dressing

- Mix mayonnaise and ketchup in a small cup until smooth.

Step four

- Combine remaining ingredients in a large bowl and toss with dressing.

Serves 10-12

GRILLED TEN

This is a great way to integrate a variety of vegetables into a meal.

INGREDIENTS

White corn	2 ears
Onion	1 large
Parsnip	1 medium
Turnip	1 medium
Zucchini	1 large
Yellow squash	1 large
Fresh fennel	1 bulb
Pepper	1 pasilla
Green bell pepper	1
Red bell pepper	1
Olive oil	1 tablespoon
Butter	2 tablespoons
Salt and pepper	to taste

Step one
- Cut kernels from corn.
- Cut all other vegetables into ⅜-inch squares.

Step two
- Heat 1 tablespoon each of olive oil and butter in a large pan.
- Add vegetables.
- Cook over high heat, stirring occasionally, for 5 minutes.
- Add salt and pepper while stirring to mix evenly.
- Add remaining 1 tablespoon of butter.
- Continue cooking for 5 minutes (a little browning is desirable).

Step three
- Place in serving dish.

Variation
Vegetables can be substituted, and not all 10 are necessary.

Serves 10

MONDAY NIGHT TORTELLINI

INGREDIENTS

Fresh mushrooms	1 pound
Prosciutto	4 oz.
Tortellini	3 packages (36 oz.)
Butter	3 tablespoons
Flour	1 tablespoon
Cream	1 pint
Parmesan cheese, freshly grated	4 oz.
Milk	1 cup
Salt	2 tablespoons

Step one
- Slice mushrooms ⅛-inch thick.
- Cut prosciutto into ⅛-by-½-inch pieces.

Step two
- About 15 minutes before serving, bring 4 quarts of water to a boil with 2 tablespoons of salt.
- Add tortellini and boil until done, 12 to 15 minutes.

Step three
- While tortellini are cooking, heat large pan over medium heat.
- Add butter, prosciutto and mushrooms and cook until mushrooms soften, approximately 5 minutes.

Step four
- Add flour and stir.

Step five
- Slowly add cream and Parmesan while stirring.
- If sauce is too thick, add milk to desired thickness.

Step six
- Combine drained tortellini with sauce in pan and serve.

Serves 10-12

BROTHERLY LOVE CHEESESTEAK

Every corner cheesesteak joint offers numerous varieties. But when it's all said and done, it's hard to beat the meat, onion, cheese combination.

INGREDIENTS

Top sirloin . . . . 3 lbs.

Onions .2 medium

French rolls or baguettes 8

American cheese. . . . . .8 slices

Olive oil . . . . .2 tablespoons

Step one

- Slice top sirloin as thinly as possible.
- Cut onions into ½-inch slices. Partially cut rolls lengthwise.

Step two

- Heat 1 tablespoon of olive oil in each of two large pans.
- Add sliced meat to one pan.
- Cook until done, approximately 10 minutes.
- Add onions to other pan.
- Sauté onions until somewhat clear, 8 to 10 minutes.

Step three

- Broil or toast rolls or baguettes while meat and onions are cooking.

Step four

- Holding rolls open-face, add slices of American cheese, meat and onions.

Variation

Other condiments, such as mustard, ketchup, peppers, pickles, etc., may be added but are not required. For true South Philly flavor, you can substitute Cheez Whiz for cheese.

Serves 8

RAZOR THIN PIZZA

INGREDIENTS

Pizza Dough:

Active-dry yeast . . . . ¼ oz. (1 envelope)

Warm water (105-115 degrees) . . . . 1 cup

Unbleached, all-purpose flour . . . . 3 cups

Salt . . . . 1 teaspoon

Olive oil . . . . .1 tablespoon

Toppings:

Fresh tomatoes . . . . 6 large

Mushrooms . . . . 1 lb.

Italian sausages 8

Grated cheese (mild cheddar and jack) . . . . 8 oz.

Step one

- Sprinkle yeast over the water and stir gently until dissolved.
- Put in warm spot for about 5 minutes.

Step two

- In a large mixing bowl, combine flour and salt.
- Make a well in the center pour the olive oil and yeast mixture into it.
- Stir until it begins to form a ball.

Step three

- Turn it out onto a clean, floured surface, dust your hands with flour and knead for about 5 minutes.

Step four

- Shape into a ball and put in a large bowl; cover and let it rise in a warm place until doubled in volume, about 1 hour.

Step five

- Press the air bubbles out of the dough, reshape into a ball and let it rise again. (You can use or refrigerate the dough at this point.)

Step six

- While dough is rising, cut tomatoes and mushrooms into ⅛-inch slices.
- In a large pan, cook sausages over medium heat until done, approximately 20 minutes.
- Let sausage cool and chop into ¼-inch pieces.

Step seven

- Divide the dough into 4 equal portions and roll each into a ball.
- Then, working on a lightly floured surface, stretch the dough and work it with your fingers and a rolling pin.

Step eight

- Preheat oven to 500 degrees.
- Transfer one piece of dough to a pizza pan or cookie sheet, add toppings and bake for 15 minutes, or until crust is golden brown and cheese is melted.
- Repeat with remaining three portions of dough.

Serves 8-10

Tip
While these classic toppings appeal to most, your potential for creativity is limitless.

POST GAME NOTES

_____
_____
_____
_____
_____
_____
_____
_____
_____
_____
_____
_____
_____
_____
_____
_____
_____
_____
_____
_____

POST GAME NOTES

It takes a good team to make a dream reality...again!

Special thanks to Stephens Press, LLC. and Ignite Design and Advertising.